Contents

Introduction	....	5
What are the Elements?	....	6
How the Periodic Table Works	....	8
Atoms	....	10
Bang! Once Upon a Time	....	12
Hydrogen	....	12
Helium	....	14
Carbon	....	16
Nitrogen	....	18
Beryllium	....	18
Lithium	....	19
Boron	....	19
Oxygen	....	20
Fluorine	....	22
Sodium	....	22
Magnesium	....	24
Aluminium	....	24
Silicon	....	25
Phosphorus	....	26
Sulphur	....	26

Chlorine	....	27
Potassium	....	28
Calcium	....	28
Scandium	....	29
Titanium	....	29
Vanadium	....	29
Chromium	....	29
Iron	....	30
Manganese	....	32
Nickel	....	32
Cobalt	....	32
Copper	....	33
Zinc	....	33
Gallium	....	33
Germanium	....	34
Arsenic	....	34
Selenium	....	34
Bromine	....	35
Rubidium	....	35
Strontium	....	35

Yttrium	....	35
Zirconium	....	35
Niobium	....	36
Molybdenum	....	36
Technetium	....	36
Ruthenium	....	36
Rhodium	....	37
Palladium	....	37
Cadmium	....	37
Silver	....	38
Indium	....	39
Tin	....	39
Antimony	....	40
Tellurium	....	40
Iodine	....	40
Caesium	....	41
Barium	....	41
The Lanthanides	....	42
Hafnium	....	44
Tantalum	....	44
Tungsten	....	44
Rhenium	....	44

Osmium	....	45
Iridium	....	45
Platinum	....	45
Gold	....	46
Mercury	....	48
Thallium	....	50
Bismuth	....	51
Astatine	....	51
Francium	....	51
Lead	....	52
Polonium	....	54
Radium	....	55
Actinium	....	56
Thorium	....	56
Protactinium	....	56
Uranium	....	57
Fictional Elements	....	58
The Quick Particle Guide	....	59
The Complete Periodic Table	....	60
Find Out More	....	61
Glossary	....	62
Index	....	63

A Beginner's GUIDE to The PERIODIC TABLE

Gill Arbuthnott

ILLUSTRATED BY Marc Mones

A & C BLACK

For Holly – Thank you!

First published 2014 by
A & C Black, an imprint of Bloomsbury Publishing Plc
50 Bedford Square, London, WC1B 3DP

www.bloomsbury.com

Bloomsbury is a registered trademark of Bloomsbury Publishing Plc

Additional picture acknowledgements:
Additional images all Shutterstock, aside from the following: p6 bottom © Wikimedia Commons,
p7 top © Wikimedia Commons, p13 top © Wikimedia Commons, p13 top © Wikimedia Commons,
p26 middle © Imperial War Museum/Wikimedia Commons, p44 top © Wikimedia Commons,
p46 top © Wikimedia Commons, p50 bottom © Wikimedia Commons, p54 top left © Wikimedia Commons,
p54 top right © Wikimedia Commons, p54 bottom © Wikimedia Commons.

ISBN 978-1-4729-0885-8

A CIP catalogue for this book is available from the British Library.

Printed in China by Leo Paper Products, Heshan, Guangdong

1 3 5 7 9 10 8 6 4 2

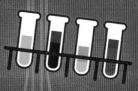

Introduction

How many different building blocks does it take to make a cell? Or a stone? Or a star? You might think it would be hundreds or even thousands, but actually it's far fewer.

But maybe that's not really such a surprise. After all, think how many different creations you can make from only a few building bricks. The 'building bricks' of the universe are called elements. There are only 92 of them, but there are millions of possible compounds you can make from them.

Have you ever wanted to know which metal screams when you bend it? Or which one is so reactive it can make glass burst into flames? Do you want to discover which are the most poisonous and which are the most radioactive elements?

Then read on...

What are the Elements?

An element is a substance that can't be broken down into a simpler substance by any sort of chemical reaction. It only contains one type of atom. There are 92 different elements that occur naturally, and some more that can only be made in a laboratory. Chemists have discovered that some of these man-made elements do actually occur naturally, but only in tiny amounts. However, we're going to stick with the original 92 in this book.

Chemists started to identify elements hundreds of years ago, and by the middle of the 1800s, 57 were known. Nobody could agree on how they should be grouped together. Someone needed to take charge and sort things out…

It was a job for Professor Mendeleev.

Dmitri Mendeleev

was born in 1834 in Siberia, the youngest of 14, or possibly even 17 children (perhaps they all kept moving around when their parents tried to count them)! When Mendeleev grew up he taught Chemistry at St Petersburg University. In photos he looks like a real mad scientist — supposedly he only cut his hair and beard once a year!

Reihen	Gruppo I. — R²O	Gruppo II. — RO	Gruppo III. — R²O³	Gruppo IV. RH⁴ RO²	Gruppo V. RH³ R²O⁵	Gruppo VI. RH² RO³	Gruppo VII. RH R²O⁷	Gruppo VIII. — RO⁴
1	H=1							
2	Li=7	Be=9,4	B=11	C=12	N=14	O=16	F=19	
3	Na=23	Mg=24	Al=27,8	Si=28	P=31	S=32	Cl=35,5	
4	K=39	Ca=40	—=44	Ti=48	V=51	Cr=52	Mn=55	Fe=56, Co=59, Ni=59, Cu=63.
5	(Cu=63)	Zn=65	—=68	—=72	As=75	Se=78	Br=80	
6	Rb=85	Sr=87	?Yt=88	Zr=90	Nb=94	Mo=96	—=100	Ru=104, Rh=104, Pd=106, Ag=108.
7	(Ag=108)	Cd=112	In=113	Sn=118	Sb=122	Te=125	J=127	
8	Cs=133	Ba=137	?Di=138	?Ce=140	—	—	—	
9	(—)	—	—	—	—	—	—	
10	—	—	?Er=178	?La=180	Ta=182	W=184	—	Os=195, Ir=197, Pt=198, Au=199.
11	(Au=199)	Hg=200	Tl=204	Pb=207	Bi=208	—	—	
12	—	—	—	Th=231	—	U=240	—	

Professor Mendeleev's periodic table.

Professor Mendeleev's chemistry class

Mendeleev had a brilliant idea during his career, and that was to arrange the elements based on their weights and their properties (how they behaved). He called his arrangement The Periodic Table.

Mendeleev found that when he arranged them in this way there seemed to be 'families' of elements that showed similarities, and gaps in the table where no known element fitted the pattern. Mendeleev predicted that new elements would be found to fill the gaps and suggested what weights and properties they would have.

This helped other chemists to find them, and Mendeleev's predictions were proved correct.

How the Periodic Table Works

Here is the modern periodic table. Let's take a closer look...

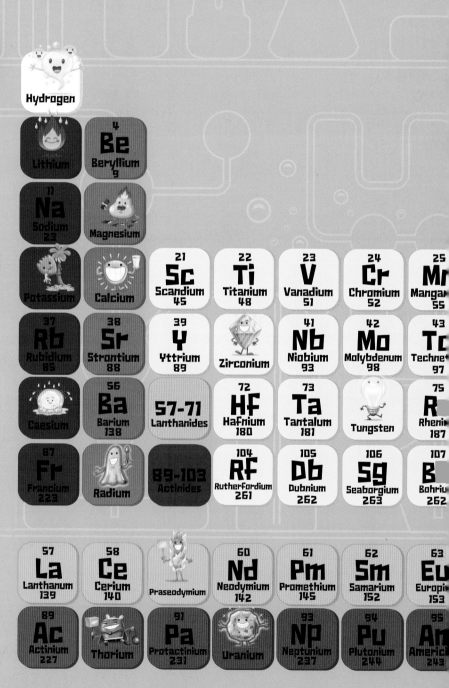

The colour of each box tells you if the element is a metal, non-metal or metalloid. The rows in the table are called periods. If you read across a period the atomic numbers of the elements increase from left to right. The columns of the table are called groups. The elements in a group have similar properties and get heavier the further down the group they are.

Each element has a box.
The box contains:

The atomic number
(The number of protons in an element)

The chemical symbol
(A one, two or three letter code for the element)

The name of the element

Atomic number 79
Au
Gold

Non-metals
- Hydrogen
- Non-metal
- Noble gases
- Metalloids or Semi-metals

Metals
- Alkali metals
- Alkali-earth metals
- Transition metals
- Rare earths
- Radioactive rare earths
- Other metals

Helium

5 **B** Boron 11	Carbon	Nitrogen	Oxygen	Fluorine	10 **Ne** Neon 20
13 **Al** Aluminium 27	Silicon	15 **P** Phosphorus 31	Sulphur	Chlorine	Argon

		28 **Ni** Nickel 58	Copper	30 **Zn** Zinc 64	31 **Ga** Gallium 69	32 **Ge** Germanium 74	Arsenic	Selenium	35 **Br** Bromine 79	36 **Kr** Krypton 84
Iron	Cobalt									
44 **Ru** Ruthenium 102	45 **Rh** Rhodium 103	46 **Pd** Palladium 106	Silver	Cadmium	Indium	50 **Sn** Tin 120	Antimony	52 **Te** Tellurium 130	53 **I** Iodine 127	54 **Xe** Xenon 132
76 **Os** Osmium 192	77 **Ir** Iridium 193	Platinum	Gold	Mercury	81 **Ti** Thallium 205	Lead	Bismuth	Polonium	85 **At** Astatine 210	86 **Rn** Radon 222
108 **Hs** Hassium 265	109 **Mt** Meitnerium 266	110 **Ds** Darmstadtium 269	111 **Rg** Roentgenium 272	112 **Cn** Copernicium 285	113 **Uut** Ununtrium 286	114 **Fl** Flerovium 289	115 **Uup** Ununpentium 289	116 **Lv** Livermonium 293	117 **Uus** Ununseptium 294	118 **Uno** Ununoctium 294

64 **Gd** Gadolinium 158	65 **Tb** Terbium 159	66 **Dy** Dysprosium 164	Holmium	68 **Er** Erbium 168	69 **Tm** Thulium 169	70 **Yb** Ytterbium 174	71 **Lu** Lutetium 175	Lanthanides
96 **Cm** Curium 247	97 **Bk** Berkelium 247	98 **Cf** Californium 251	99 **Es** Einsteinium 254	100 **Fm** Fermium 257	101 **Md** Mendelevium 258	102 **No** Nobelium 255	103 **Lr** Lawrencium 256	Actinides

*There is a full periodic table on page 60 which contains all the chemical symbols.

Atoms

An atom is the smallest unit of an element and it is made up of protons, neutrons and electrons. Atoms are incredibly small – 0.000001 milimetres – and can only be seen by using a very special microscope. Their tiny size is very hard to imagine, and what makes it even harder is that most of that is empty space!

The nucleus (the centre) of an atom is made up of protons and neutrons. These make up almost all of the atom's mass. Protons have a positive charge, and the electrons whizzing round outside the nucleus have an equal negative charge. Neutrons don't have a charge.

☢ If the whole atom was the size of a football stadium, the nucleus would be the size of a marble, and the electrons would be like tiny insects buzzing round the edge. The rest is just... nothing!

Here's how atoms are often shown:

electrons

nucleus

Let's try and understand this a different way...

Compounds and mixtures

Most substances in the world are compounds or mixtures. Compounds are made up of atoms of two or more elements joined together to form molecules. For instance, a molecule of water is an oxygen atom joined to two hydrogen atoms.

Air, on the other hand, is a mixture. It is made up of various elements like oxygen and nitrogen, together with compounds like carbon dioxide, all bobbing about together without actually being joined to each other.

Think of a mixture, like air, as a box of building bricks – they're in the box, but they're not joined together. A compound, like water, would be building bricks joined to each other.

Solids, liquids and gases

These are what are known as the States of Matter. Chemists used to think that there were only three – solids, liquids and gases – and most things exist in one of these forms. However, there is a fourth reasonably common one called plasma (not the same as the stuff in your blood), and a whole load of what are called Exotic States of Matter that only exist in extreme laboratory conditions, or are just theoretical.

But lets get back to the basics...

Solids have a fixed shape and volume. The molecules are tightly packed meaning that they can't move around – but they do vibrate.

Liquids have a fixed volume, but take the shape of the container they are in. The molecules are tightly packed but can move a bit more than they can in a solid.

Gases have no fixed volume or shape. The molecules are not tightly packed and can move around freely.

Bang! Once Upon a Time...

Once upon a time, there was no universe at all, no space, no time – nothing. Then, a tiny, unbelievably hot and dense thing called a singularity appeared.

Eventually, about 13.7 billion years ago, the singularity suddenly exploded with indescribable force, and began to expand incredibly fast, in what physicists now call the Big Bang. As the singularity expanded, becoming less hot and dense, space and time came into existence and the universe was born. And it's still expanding now – galaxies are continuously moving away from each other. At that point in time, there were no elements – let alone stars or planets – just subatomic particles (loads of things that eventually form an atom). It took hundreds of thousands of years for the first atoms to form, then eventually, the first elements: hydrogen and helium – let's start with them and work our way from the lightest to the heaviest elements in the periodic table.

Atomic number 1

H

Hydrogen
Non-Metal

Hydrogen is the lightest element – its atoms each contain only one proton and one electron. It is also the most common element. At least 90% of all the atoms in the universe are hydrogen.

It was one of the first elements created by the Big Bang. Hydrogen is lighter than air, so was previously used to fill balloons and airships for air travel. Now we are beginning to use burning hydrogen as a fuel in buses, as it only produces water when it is burned, instead of the pollutants produced by burning fossil fuels.

The Hindenberg disaster

Airships filled with hydrogen were known as zeppelins. They were regularly being used to carry passengers by 1910 and were used by the German army to bomb London during World War I. Transatlantic passenger flights started in the 1920s but on May 6, 1937, disaster struck when the Hindenberg airship burned and crashed in New Jersey after flying from Frankfurt, killing 35 of the 97 people on board. It was the end of airship travel. It was assumed for a long time that the crash was caused by burning hydrogen, but now there are other theories. One of these is that flammable paint on the airship 'skin' was the first thing to catch fire, with the hydrogen burning later.

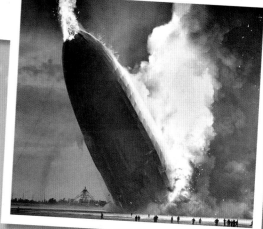

Crash of the *Hindenburg* in New Jersey, May 1937.

Burning stars

The sun is mostly made of hydrogen. Sunlight? That's the visible energy released when hydrogen is turned into helium by a process called nuclear fusion, which releases huge amounts of energy.

Atomic number 2

He

Helium
Non-Metal

Helium was identified in space before it was found on Earth, in 1882 by a scientist studying lava from Vesuvius. It was created in the Big Bang and is lighter than air, which is why helium party balloons float.

Although it is the second most abundant element in the universe, making up almost a quarter of its mass, it's quite rare on Earth – most of it comes from natural gas – and in fact we are running out of it! The molecules are so tiny that whenever any is released, it just floats off into space. Helium is also used in the manufacture of mobile phones and computer chips, as a super coolant in the Large Hadron Collider, and as part of the gas mixture breathed by deep-sea divers.

Breathing helium

If you have a helium party balloon ask an adult if you can try the following experiment.

🎈 Untie the balloon carefully, breathe out, then take a breath of helium from the balloon. Now try talking and you'll find your voice has gone very squeaky!

🎈 Make sure you breathe normal air for a few minutes before you try it again so you don't get dizzy.

Why does your voice change? It's because the sound waves made by your vocal cords vibrating are travelling through helium, not air, and because helium is much lighter than air, they travel faster.

The Noble Gases

Non-metals

These are the elements in the same column or group of the periodic table as **helium**.

They are

Neon	Ne	Atomic number 10
Argon	Ar	Atomic number 18
Krypton	Kr	Atomic number 36
Xenon	Xe	Atomic number 54
Radon	Rn	Atomic number 86

10
Ne
Neon

18
Ar
Argon

Kr
Krypton

54
Xe
Xenon

86
Rn
Radon

They are called the Noble Gases, because they are so unreactive – they don't like to have anything to do with any other elements. In fact neon doesn't form any chemical compounds at all. They should really be called the Stuck Up Gases!

They are used in various sorts of lighting. Argon was used in old-fashioned light bulbs and is still used in fluorescent tubes.

The gases have medical uses too – xenon is used as an anaesthetic and radioactive radon is used as a cancer treatment.

Krypton and Kryptonite

Don't confuse krypton with Kryptonite! Kryptonite, which drains Superman of his powers, is a fictional element from Superman's home planet, Krypton. As far as we know krypton is just a gas, not a planet!

Atomic number 6

C
Carbon
Non-Metal

All life on Earth is based on chemicals that contain carbon. It can join with other elements to form millions of different compounds. Pure carbon can exist in several different forms: graphite (which is the 'lead' in lead pencils), diamond, the wonderfully named 'buckyballs' (which are minute spheres of graphite), and graphene (which is a one atom thick layer of graphite). Scientists are very excited about graphene because it's strong, light, almost transparent, and conducts both heat and electricity very well.

> The scientific name of the diamond star is BPM 37093. What a mouthful!

Diamond

Diamond is the hardest naturally occurring material and most diamonds are mined in Africa. The largest diamond ever found was the Cullinan, which weighed over 600 grams! It was cut into over 100 smaller diamonds, some of which are part of the Crown Jewels.

The diamond star

Astronomers have found the remains of a massive star, which has been transformed into a huge diamond – a diamond that may be five times the size of the Earth!

Global warming

Fossil fuels (coal, gas and oil) were originally living things, so contain lots of carbon. When we burn them, they release carbon dioxide gas, which collects in the atmosphere and traps extra heat from the sun there. This is known as the Greenhouse Effect, and many scientists are worried that it is leading to climate change.

Recipe for a human

Which elements are you made of? And how much of them do you need to make a human?

A 70 kilogram adult is mostly made of:

O	43kg oxygen
C	16kg carbon
H	7kg hydrogen
N	1.8kg nitrogen
Ca	1kg calcium
P	780g phosphorus
K	140g potassium
S	140g sulphur
	100g sodium
Cl	95g chlorine
Mg	19g magnesium
Fe	4.2g iron
F	2.6g fluorine
Zn	2.3g zinc
Si	1.0g silicon

Atomic number 7

N
Nitrogen
Non-Metal

Almost 80% of the air around us is made up of nitrogen. We breathe it in and out, but we don't use it for anything in our bodies. It is vital for plant growth, but is often in short supply in its useable forms, so modern farming relies on adding artificially produced nitrate fertiliser to soil, so that plants can grow well.

Liquid nitrogen has a temperature of –196 degrees Celsius. If you put a banana into liquid nitrogen it will freeze so hard that you can use it to hammer a nail into a plank of wood! It is used (liquid nitrogen, that is, not a frozen banana) as a refrigerant to preserve embryos for in vitro fertilisation.

Laughing gas

Laughing gas is nitrous oxide. It was used as an anaesthetic to relieve pain without knocking the patient out. Although many people found it made them sleepy, it also gave some people the giggles, hence its name. In the 1800s rich people sometimes had laughing gas parties because of the enjoyable effects it caused.

Explosives

Dynamite was invented by Alfred Nobel in 1866 and the money he made from it funds the Nobel Prizes – including, ironically, the Nobel Peace Prize! Nitro-glycerine is a highly explosive liquid. TNT is used in armour piercing shells. Azide is an explosive that saves lives – it's what makes car airbags inflate so quickly. All these explosives contain different compounds of nitrogen.

Atomic number 4

Be
Beryllium
Metal

This is only generated by exploding supernovae (giant exploding stars), so not very common at all. It can be found as crystals of the ore beryllium, up to six metres long!

Atomic number 3

Li
Lithium
Metal

This was the third element created by the Big Bang. It's the lightest metal, and is very reactive – because of this it has to be stored under oil or coated in petroleum jelly as it can burst into flame when it comes into contact with water and oxygen. Lithium carbonate is an important treatment for some mental health problems.

Atomic number 5

B
Boron
Non-Metal

Boron is the lightest metalloid, and its mixture of properties gives it many uses. Without boron, there would be no Silly Putty, Queen Elizabeth I wouldn't have had her white complexion, and we'd be missing one colour of green from fireworks. Boron is always found combined with other elements, and although it has been used for hundreds of years, it wasn't until 1892 that Ezekiel Weintraub managed to isolate it.

Home made Silly Putty

Ask a grown up to help you make your own Silly Putty using this recipe!

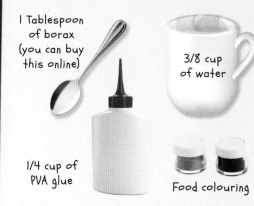

1 Tablespoon of borax (you can buy this online)

3/8 cup of water

1/4 cup of PVA glue

Food colouring

• Dissolve the borax in 1/8 cup of water.

• Slowly mix the rest of the water into the glue and add a few drops of food colouring.

• Stir the two mixtures together. If it's too sticky, add a little more borax until it's stiff enough.

• Store in a sealed plastic container in the fridge or it will go mouldy!

• Silly Putty flows like a liquid but bounces like a rubber ball.

19

Atomic number 8

O
Oxygen
Non-Metal

The most common element on Earth, Oxygen makes up 20% of every breath you take. It's needed in order to burn fuel like coal, gas or petrol so they can release the energy they contain. This happens in your body too. The oxygen you breathe in is used in all your cells to release energy from the food you eat.

When Earth first formed, there was no oxygen in the atmosphere. It wasn't until plants evolved and began to produce it by the process of photosynthesis that most of it was made.

Here are some things I bet you didn't know about oxygen.

Sun

Ozone layer

Earth

Ozone: Goody or baddy?

Most oxygen molecules are made of two oxygen atoms, but some are made of three. These are called ozone molecules and they create a thin layer of ozone about 20 kilometres above Earth. This protects us by absorbing over 90% of the harmful UV radiation in sunlight. In recent years the ozone layer has been getting thinner due to man-made pollution. However, the damage seems to be slowing down now that some of the chemicals involved have been banned. So ozone must be a goody then?

Not always. Low-level ozone is definitely a baddy. It can worsen asthma and bronchitis and damage the surface of the lungs. It also damages plant leaves.

Northern Lights

Also known as the Aurora Borealis, these are spectacular bands of light that appear in Northern skies in the right atmospheric conditions. They show up as green or crimson 'curtains' of light when cosmic rays interact with oxygen molecules in the outer atmosphere, and move about as the rays are pulled around by the Earth's magnetic field. The best places to see them are Iceland, Greenland and northern Scandinavia, but you can also see them from the north of Scotland.

Northern Lights, Iceland.

Stevie Wonder

The American singer-songwriter Stevie Wonder has been blind since shortly after birth. It's reported that this is because when he was born prematurely he was given extra oxygen. Unfortunately, high concentrations of oxygen can cause abnormal growth of the blood vessels in the retina at the back of the eye, and in his case it caused him to go blind.

F
Fluorine
Non-Metal

Pure fluorine is a pale yellow gas, but it's always found as part of compounds in nature. There are things containing fluorine all over your house, but you wouldn't want to meet it as fluorine gas, which is so reactive that it will make almost anything – even glass – burst into flames.

You'll meet it as fluoride, in your toothpaste, where it helps keep your teeth strong (though too much will turn them brown). Some waterproof materials used to make rain jackets are made using fluorine as well.

Na
Sodium
Metal

Sodium compounds give the sea its salty taste and we use sodium chloride (salt) as our favourite food flavouring. Sodium is needed for our nerves to work. Part of the Roman soldier's wage was money to buy salt and this is where the word 'salary' comes from.

Salinas Grandes, Salt desert, Argentina Andes.

Crystals

Crystals are solids where molecules are arranged in a highly organised 3D pattern. Crystals include sodium chloride – in other words, salt-diamonds and snowflakes. Crystals have flat faces called facets, with sharp edges. Why not grow your own?

Unfortunately, you can't grow diamonds so easily.

Growing salt crystals

You will need:

1/4 cup of salt

1 cup of boiling water

A piece of sponge (bath not cake!)

2 teaspoons of vinegar

Food colouring (optional)

• Get an adult to help you mix the boiling water, salt, vinegar and food colouring (if using) and stir well.

• Put the sponge in a shallow dish.

• Pour enough mixture over the sponge in order to soak it completely and cover the bottom of the dish. Keep the rest for later.

• Leave the dish on a windowsill or somewhere warm and airy. Crystals should start to form within 24 hours.

• As the liquid in the dish evaporates, add more mixture and see how big you can get the crystals to grow.

Atomic number 12

Mg

Magnesium
Metal

Plants need magnesium to be able to photosynthesise (make their own food) and we need it to prevent our bones from becoming brittle. Plants take in magnesium compounds from soil through their roots, but obviously we can't do the same and so we have to eat it. The good news? Chocolate is a good source of magnesium!

Magnesium burns with an intense white light and was once used in photographic flashbulbs. It was also used in the firebombs that were dropped on cities during World War II.

Atomic number 13

Al

Aluminium
Metal

Aluminium is the most common metal on Earth, but when it was first discovered in the 1800s it was more expensive than gold. This was because it was very difficult to purify from the minerals in which it was found. Now that an easy method has been discovered to isolate it, aluminium is used to make everything from soft drink cans to car bodies to racing bikes because it's very light.

It's also a good conductor of heat, which is why it's used in cooking foil, and a good reflector of heat, which is why it's used in spacecraft. It's a very good idea to recycle it, because it takes a lot of energy to make it.

Atomic number 14

Si
Silicon
Non-Metal

Most soil and rock has lots of silicon in it. Lots of precious and semi-precious stones such as emerald, jade and amethyst also contain silicon. Silicon is used to make everything from bricks and glass to silicon chips and solar cells.

Silicon chips

Silicon chips control everything from your phone, to your computer, to your microwave. They are sometimes called 'integrated circuits' and were a huge step forward from conventional electronic circuits because they could be made much smaller and were much cheaper. This meant that very complex circuits only took up a tiny space. The first silicon integrated circuit was developed in 1959.

Arrowheads

In the Stone Age, knives and arrowheads were made from flint – a compound of silicon and oxygen that could be split to give very sharp edges.

Silicon chip for a computer.

Today's chips can contain millions of times more information than the early versions.

Atomic number 15

P
Phosphorus
Non-Metal

This was the first element to be discovered in modern times and was first isolated from human urine by a German alchemist who was trying to make the Philosopher's Stone. It's highly toxic, but there is lots of it in your body in the form of calcium phosphate, which is the main ingredient of bones and teeth. It's very reactive, which is why it's used to make match heads.

Atomic number 16

S
Sulphur
Non-Metal

Sulphur is a bright yellow non-metal made in volcanic eruptions, both on land and on the seabed. It used to be called Brimstone (which means 'burnstone'). This is why sulphur is also associated with the devil. Sulphur itself doesn't smell, but lots of sulphur compounds do – they give garlic, mustard, cabbage and skunks their smell.

Operation Hamburg after the bombing of Gomorrah.

In World War II, tons of burning phosphorus was dropped on Hamburg by the Allies (the countries who fought against Nazi Germany), destroying most of the city in Operation Gomorrah.

Skunk smell

This can temporarily blind you. It makes your eyes water, and can cause nausea and breathing difficulties in people with asthma. It's very difficult to get rid of the smell. Because of this people drive round dead skunks, not over them!

Sulphur medicines

These have been used for hundreds of years. Brimstone and treacle was a popular Victorian laxative, and sulphonamide drugs are still used to treat gut infections.

Gunpowder

Gunpowder is a mixture of sulphur, charcoal and saltpetre (potassium nitrate). When it was first made, it had to be bashed into a powder by people with hammers. Not a great job, as it would often explode. Now, gunpowder is mainly used in fireworks.

Mustard gas

Mustard gas is a deadly poisonous gas that contains sulphur. It's easy to make and use, and damages cells lining the lungs. Mustard gas was used during World War I.

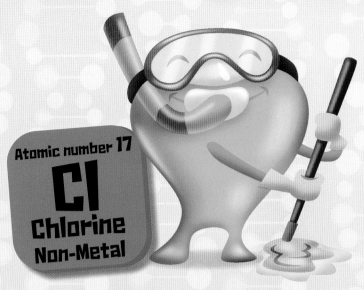

Atomic number 17
Cl
Chlorine
Non-Metal

Chlorine was originally given the much less snappy name of 'dephlogisticated muriatic acid air' when it was described in the 1630s. However, it had been known and used for thousands of years – most commonly in the form of sodium chloride (salt).

Most disinfectants and bleaches are chlorine compounds, and drinking water in many countries is treated with chlorine to kill microbes, helping to wipe out diseases like typhoid and cholera. However, it can also be deadly. Chlorine gas was used as a poison in the trenches of World War I, killing over 5000 soldiers.

Atomic number 19

K

Potassium

Metal

Why K? It's from the medieval Latin word kalium, for ash from which potassium was first isolated.

It has many uses, including being used as a fertiliser and meat preservative. It's vital for nerves to work properly. If you sweat a lot, you can lose so much potassium that you get cramps and muscle weakness. However, you can easily replace the missing potassium by eating a banana, which is why they are the snack of choice for many tennis players.

Atomic number 20

Ca

Calcium

Metal

Calcium is a silvery metal, but most of the things you will come across that contain calcium are white, for example, chalk, bones, teeth or the white cliffs of Dover. Bones and teeth are made of calcium phosphate whereas the cliffs (and chalk) are made from calcium carbonate, and are the skeletons of billions of tiny, long-dead organisms.

The expression 'stealing the limelight' meant taking attention away from another actor by standing in the light.

Lighting in the theatre used to be created by burning calcium oxide in a jet of hydrogen. Because calcium oxide is sometimes called 'lime' this was called 'limelight'.

Atomic number 21

Sc
Scandium
Metal

This is one of the elements that Mendeleev predicted should exist. Ten years after his prediction, it was discovered, but it wasn't until 1937 that someone managed to produce a lump of it, as it only occurs in trace amounts in the Earth's crust. Adding tiny amounts to aluminium makes a very strong alloy, which is used in aircraft.

Atomic number 22

Ti
Titanium
Metal

This is a very strong, but light metal, and won't rust away in seawater like iron. Because of this it is often used to make submarine hulls. It is also used to make replacement hip joints, and the pins and plates that are sometimes used to mend broken bones. It is named after the Titans – a race of giants – in Greek mythology.

Atomic number 23

V
Vanadium
Metal

Another very strong but light metal, it was used in the steel alloy that was used to manufacture the first mass-produced car, the Model T Ford.

Atomic number 24

Cr
Chromium
Metal

Chromium is a silvery white metal, but it's what gives emeralds and rubies their colours. It's used as a corrosion-proof plating on steel and used to give classic cars – especially American ones – their shiny bumpers.

Model T Ford.

Fe
Iron
Metal

Iron is the most widely used metal. The Iron Age began 3000 years ago when people learned to smelt iron from iron ore, or possibly from meteorites. Blacksmiths were regarded as almost magical because it seemed as if they could turn rock into metal.

Here are some more amazing facts about iron.

King Arthur

In the legend of King Arthur, he proves he is the rightful king by 'drawing forth the sword from the stone and anvil'. This is usually shown as him freeing a sword stuck through a big stone and a blacksmith's anvil. However, some people think this refers to forging a sword from a stone (meteorite) on an anvil — so maybe King Arthur was a blacksmith!

Rust

Iron is very reactive. One unwelcome result of this is that it will corrode if it is not protected by painting or galvanising it (coating with zinc). This corrosion is called rust, and is a compound called hydrated iron oxide. You can see this process for yourself if you put an iron or steel nail in a dish of water. It should start to rust in a few days.

Blood

In your blood there are millions of tiny red blood cells. They are full of a chemical called haemoglobin, which allows the cells to carry oxygen. Haemoglobin contains iron.

If you don't get enough iron in your diet, your blood can't carry enough oxygen.

31

Atomic number 25

Mn
Manganese
Metal

Most manganese is found on the seabed in the form of nodules – lumps of manganese minerals that form around a central particle in the same way that a pearl forms round a piece of grit. It is used in glass making to remove iron compounds and as a result creates very clear glass. It was used many thousands of years ago by the earliest artists, as the black colour in cave paintings is manganese oxide.

Atomic number 28

Ni
Nickel
Metal

Nickel is one of the four magnetic elements (the others are iron, cobalt and gadolinium). It's often used in coins, which is why the American five-cent coin is known as a nickel. It's also used to make cheap jewellery, especially earrings, but some people can become allergic to it.

> The nodules of manganese are the size of potatoes.

Atomic number 27

Co
Cobalt
Metal

This is named after the German word for goblin – kobald – because the 16th century German miners who discovered it thought it was cursed! Cobalt chloride can be used to make invisible ink. You write a secret message in invisible ink, then write a 'fake' letter on top of it with ordinary ink. When you heat the paper, the invisible message appears, as if by magic…

Cobalt

Atomic number 29

Cu
Copper
Metal

Copper has been used for thousands of years, often made into alloys with other metals. The Bronze Age was named after the alloy of copper and tin, which was used to make weapons, coins and jewellery. Now it is used in electrical wires and printed circuit boards. It is used a lot in building, as it weathers to a green finish known as verdigris. The best known example of this is probably the Statue of Liberty in New York.

Atomic number 31

Ga
Gallium
Metal

This is a metal which melts at under 30 degrees Celsius, so you could hold it in your hand and watch it melt! Chemists who like practical jokes have been known to make teaspoons out of it, which melt when you stir your tea. It is also used in mobile phones and computers. Gallium nitride is the 'blue' in Blu-ray discs.

Atomic number 30

Zn
Zinc
Metal

Zinc is vital for health, and according to research, two billion people don't get enough of it. In areas where there isn't enough zinc in the soil, crops don't grow properly. Maple syrup is a very rich source.

Bring on the pancakes!

Atomic number 32

Ge
Germanium
Metalloid

Metalloid Germanium is named after Germany and is another element which Mendeleev predicted would be found. It was first discovered in silver ore, and can be extracted during production of zinc from ore. It was used as one of the first semi-conductors. It is sold in some countries as a nutritional supplement in its inorganic form, even though it is actually harmful!

Atomic number 33

As
Arsenic
Metalloid

Highly toxic, but was used in a medicine called Salvarsen to treat parasitic blood infections. It has long been used as a poison. For many years, people thought that the French Emperor Napoleon was deliberately poisoned, because traces of arsenic were found in his hair after his death. Now it looks as though he was murdered by his wallpaper! When he was in exile on the island of St Helena, the green wallpaper in his bedroom was made using a dye that contained arsenic. When it got damp, it gave off arsenic-containing gas.

Atomic number 34

Se
Selenium
Non-Metal

Selenium is silvery and shiny, just like lots of metals, but it is a non-metal. Its name comes from the Greek word 'selene' meaning the moon. You are most likely to come across it in the much less exotic surroundings of your bathroom, where it is used in anti-dandruff shampoos.

Napoleon Bonaparte

Atomic number 35

Br
Bromine
Non-Metal

Its name means 'stench' in Greek and pure bromine is a liquid at room temperature. It's usually found in the form of bromine salts in seawater and some mineral springs. If you were very rich in ancient times, you might have your clothes dyed Tyrian purple, using a bromine-containing pigment extracted from a type of sea snail. Yuck!

Atomic number 38

Sr
Strontium
Metal

Named after the Scottish village of Strontian, where it was discovered. It has a very harmful radioactive isotope, strontium-90. Huge areas were contaminated with this by the Chernobyl nuclear disaster in Russia in 1986.

Atomic number 39

Y
Yttrium
Metal

Used when making lasers and superconductors, and in cancer treatments. The isotope yttrium-90 can be used to make needles that are more precise than surgical scalpels and can be used in delicate spinal surgery.

Atomic number 37

Rb
Rubidium
Metal

Rubidium is such a reactive metal that if you don't store it under oil, it will burst into flames in air. It is mildly radioactive and can be used to give a purple colour to fireworks.

Atomic number 40

Zr
Zirconium
Metal

If you want to buy a diamond, but can't afford it, this is the next best thing. Zirconium dioxide forms crystals that, to most people, look just like diamonds, even though zirconium itself is a soft grey metal.

Atomic number 41

Nb
Niobium
Metal

This metal can be used to make commemorative coins in lots of different colours by reacting niobium with oxygen. The Native American Full Moon coins produced in Canada in 2011 are each unique because of the way this was done.

Atomic number 42

Mo
Molybdenum
Metal

Confusingly, the name comes from the Greek word for Lead, because its ore used to get confused with lead ore. It was used in armour plating on tanks in World War I.

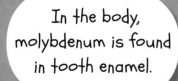

In the body, molybdenum is found in tooth enamel.

Atomic number 43

Tc
Technetium
Metal

This is one of Mendeleev's 'missing elements' and chemists searched for it for years. After many false alarms, its existence was finally confirmed in 1936. It is a radioactive metal, mostly made inside nuclear reactors. It is used in several types of medical imaging such as the SPECT scan.

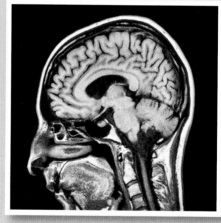

SPECT scan.

Atomic number 44

Ru
Ruthenium
Metal

One of the rarest metals on Earth. It is very resistant to corrosion, so is sometimes used as very thin plating on much cheaper metals. It may soon be used in solar cells and as part of data storage systems on hard discs.

Atomic number 46

Pd
Palladium
Metal

Like rhodium, this silvery-white metal is used in catalytic converters. It is also used to make an alloy of gold – white gold – for use in jewellery.

Atomic number 48

Cd
Cadmium
Metal

You might have rechargeable batteries in your house that contain nickel and cadmium, though they are now being replaced by less toxic ones. Cadmium is hugely toxic to humans and to the environment. On the other hand, without it, Claude Monet couldn't have painted his awesome pictures. One of his favourite colours was cadmium yellow.

Atomic number 45

Rh
Rhodium
Metal

Almost 80% of the rhodium that is produced worldwide is used in catalytic converters, which make the emissions from car engines much less damaging to the environment. It is also a precious metal, and is sometimes used to symbolise great wealth or honour. Paul McCartney was given a rhodium plated disc by the Guinness Book of World Records in 1979 in recognition of the fact that he was the bestselling recording artist and songwriter of all time.

Paul McCartney

Atomic number 47
Ag
Silver
Metal

Silver was first used in Egypt over 5000 years ago. Since its discovery it has been used for a variety of different things, for example mirrors and jewellery. It was used in photographic film (before digital cameras) because silver salts are light-sensitive and change to silver when exposed to light. This made a pattern of light and dark, which could be processed into a black and white photograph. Light-sensitive silver salts are now used in photo reactive glasses – the kind that get darker in sunlight.

Mirrors

Mirrors were originally sheets of polished metal, like bronze or sometimes silver. 'Looking glasses' were first used in the Middle Ages and were made from glass with silver foil behind them. Now the silver is chemically bonded to the glass to make modern mirrors more durable.

Silver nitrate

Previously this was used as an antiseptic, as silver is deadly to many bacteria and viruses. It is now put in some paints to make antibacterial surfaces.

Silver linings in clouds

'Every cloud has a silver lining' just might be true... Silver iodide is dropped from aircraft or fired from rockets into clouds in 'cloud seeding', a method of trying to produce rain.

Indium is used in LCD screens.

Atomic number 49

In
Indium
Metal

Not named after India, but after the Latin word for indigo. It's used in LCD televisions, liquid crystals and solar cells, and it's running out fast. We may only have 20 years supply left. Weirdly – if you bend a piece of indium, it screams! It's the crystals rearranging themselves.

Atomic number 50

Sn
Tin
Metal

This metal screams as well, if you break a bar of it. It's used for coating steel to make tin cans because it doesn't get corroded by acidic food. In Britain, most tin was mined in Cornwall, but the last tin mine closed in 1998. Pewter is an alloy of lead and tin which was widely used for tankards and plates until the 19th century.

Atomic number 52

Te
Tellurium
Metalloid

Very rare on Earth, but used to make DVD and Blu-ray discs. It's toxic, and someone poisoned with tellurium has breath that smells of garlic (but then, so does someone who has been eating garlic!).

Atomic number 51

Sb
Antimony
Metalloid

Antimony is toxic and was often used to get rid of inconvenient relatives in the 19th century. Some people think that it was used to poison the composer Mozart in 1791. If you get the dose right though, it can be used as a laxative. In the Middle Ages, antimony pills could be bought as re-useable laxatives: you swallowed one, then waited for it to reappear! Yuck!

Mozart

Atomic number 53

I
Iodine
Non-Metal

Iodine compounds can be isolated easily from seawater. It is vital for humans and many other animals. It is needed by the body to make chemicals which help control how food is broken down to release energy. Nowadays it is added to salt, but previously the only way to get enough was by eating sea fish. Before refrigerated transport, this meant that if you lived a long way from the sea, you probably didn't get enough. The iodine is used in the thyroid gland in your neck, to make important chemical messengers. If you don't get enough, this gland grows extra big, leading to a condition called goitre.

Atomic number 55

Cs

Caesium
Metal

This is a spectacularly reactive element that explodes in water, and has to be stored under oil and handled in a non-reactive atmosphere. Large quantities of Cs-137, the radioactive isotope, were released into the atmosphere by the Chernobyl nuclear explosion. It spread on the wind across huge areas of Europe, contaminating soil and affecting livestock. However caesium does have its uses. If you want to know the time really accurately, consult an atomic clock, many of which depend on atomic changes in caesium to work.

If you were a witch in the middle ages, what you really needed to impress other witches were some Bologna stones. These were pebbles which, if you left them in the sun for a day, would glow in the dark for days afterwards. These stones contained barite, a compound of barium. Barium is used in 'barium meals' for showing up the stomach and intestines in medical scans.

Atomic number 56

Ba

Barium
Metal

41

The Lanthanides

The lanthanides are a group of elements that live in a sort of 'annexe' at the bottom of the periodic table. They share many properties, and are found in the same areas. Many of them were discovered in samples of rock near the village of Ytterby in Sweden.

Atomic number 57
Lt
Lanthanum
Metal

Lanthanum metal is never found in its pure form. It took a hundred years for someone to work out how to purify it. Among its many uses are making nickel-hydride batteries for hybrid cars and clearing unwanted algae from ponds.

Atomic number 58
Ce
Cerium
Metal

Cerium looks a bit like iron, but is much softer. Shavings of cerium will burst into flames in contact with air. Cerium is used in catalytic converters.

Atomic number 59
Pr
Praseodymium
Metal

It can be used to colour glass and enamel yellow and is part of a special glass that can slow the speed of light to a few hundred metres per second instead of 299,792,458 metres per second.

SLOW

Atomic number 60
Nd
Neodymium
Metal

Neodymium magnets are the strongest magnets you can get. A neodymium magnet can lift 1000 times its own weight.

Atomic number 61
Pm
Promethium
Metal

This is highly radioactive, so hardly ever occurs naturally, although it can be made in a lab. It can be used to make luminous paint.

Atomic number 62
Sm
Samarium
Metal

Discovered by the fabulously named Paul Emile Lecoq de Boisbaudran in 1879. Radioactive samarium-153 is used in the treatment of some cancers.

Atomic number 63
Eu
Europium
Metal

Named after the continent, of course. It doesn't have many uses now, but was vital for making early colour televisions.

Atomic number 64
Gd
Gadolinium
Metal

It's very good at absorbing neutrons, so it is used for shielding in nuclear reactors. It is magnetic, but only up to 19 degrees Celsius.

Atomic number 65
Tb
Terbium
Metal

Pure terbium is soft, silvery-white and very expensive – four times as costly as platinum. Its most interesting use is to make the device called the SoundBug. This is a small speaker that can transform an entire flat surface like metal or wood into a speaker when it is attached to it.

Atomic number 66
Dy
Dysprosium
Metal

Its name means 'hard to get' – and it is. Although it's a metal, it's so soft you can cut it with an ordinary knife. It's needed to make motors for electric cars, among other things, and it may run out as soon as 2015!

Atomic number 67
Ho
Holmium
Metal

Holmium is named after the city of Stockholm. It has the highest magnetic strength of any element and is used in nuclear control rods.

Atomic number 68
Er
Erbium
Metal

Erbium reacts so easily with water or oxygen that it's never found as a pure metal. Your dentist might be using it if you have laser dentistry.

Atomic number 69
Tm
Thulium
Metal

Although it is a metal, Thulium will catch on fire at a lower temperature than paper! It is used in portable x-ray machines.

Atomic number 70
Yb
Ytterbium
Metal

Most is extracted from clay in some areas of China, but it is named after the village of Ytterby in Sweden, where it was first found. Used in pressure gauges that measure explosions and earthquakes.

Atomic number 71
Lu
Lutetium
Metal

This is a very hard, dense metal which, for a long time, was the most costly element to isolate. It is still too rare and expensive to have many uses.

The rocket nozzle of the Apollo Lunar Module contains Hafnium.

Atomic number 74
W
Tungsten
Metal

Also known as Wolfram, which means wolf froth! It is the heaviest element with a biological function – it is used by some bacteria. Until recently it was used for the wire filament in light bulbs.

Atomic number 72
HF
Hafnium
Metal

Hafnium was one of the last stable elements to be identified, because its chemical properties are so similar to zirconium that scientists found it very difficult to tell them apart. It is used for control rods in pressurised water reactors.

Atomic number 73
Ta
Tantalum
Metal

Because it is corrosion resistant, it is sometimes used to make parts for very expensive watches. It is named after Tantalus, a figure in Greek mythology, who was punished after his death by having food and drink constantly just out of reach.

Atomic number 75
Re
Rhenium
Metal

It was the last stable element to be discovered, in 1925 – not surprising, since the scientists concerned had to process 660 kilograms of molybdenite ore to get one gram of it. Used in superalloys to make jet engine parts.

Atomic number 76

Os
Osmium
Metal

Osmium is the densest element and hardest metal. It is named after the Greek word 'osme' which means smell, so it's really called Smellium! It is used in electron microscopy and is the least abundant stable element in the Earth's crust.

Atomic number 77

Ir
Iridium
Metal

Rare on Earth, but common in meteorites, including the one that some scientists think may have led to the extinction of the dinosaurs. A meteorite around ten kilometres wide crashed to Earth in the Gulf of Mexico near the Yucatan peninsula, leaving a crater about 300 kilometres wide. It left an iridium-rich layer of clay. When the meteorite struck, it sent up a huge dust cloud that blocked so much sunlight that most plants could no longer photosynthesise. The animals – including dinosaurs – which depended on these plants died out.

Atomic number 78

Pt
Platinum
Metal

Platinum is a precious metal – even more precious than gold, and it has been used to make jewellery for at least 2000 years. Interestingly, although there were silver and gold rushes, there was never a platinum rush, even though you can find it in some river sands, like gold. The International Prototype Kilogram (which defines exactly what a kilogram is) is a cylinder of platinum-iridium alloy made in 1879. A record that sells more than one million copies has 'gone platinum'. Platinum is used in catalytic converters, electrodes, and in cancer treatments.

Atomic number 79

Au
Gold
Metal

The symbol comes from the Latin word for gold – aurum. Most other metals are silver in colour, but gold is gold coloured because its electrons move so fast.

Gold is one of the rarest elements on Earth. Most of it exists in seawater, but it is too dispersed to be collected. It is popular for jewellery because it stays bright and untarnished indefinitely. The biggest nugget of gold ever found was the Welcome Stranger, mined in Victoria, Australia in 1858, and weighing in at an impressive 72.04 kilograms. It was melted down in London in 1859.

Here are some more nuggets of information about gold.

The California Gold Rush

This took place between 1848 and 1855, and brought 300,000 people to California. San Francisco was a village of 200 people when it started and by 1852, it was a city of 36,000. However, this wasn't the only gold rush. They also took place in Alaska, Australia and South Africa.

Preparing the fields for the gold extraction.

Panning for gold

This is a very ancient way of extracting gold from river gravel. Water is swirled over the gravel in a special shallow pan. The lighter bits are washed out, but because gold is so heavy, it stays at the bottom of the pan. You can even pan for gold in parts of the UK!

The legend of the Golden Fleece

One of the Greek myths is about how the hero Jason stole the Golden Fleece. Some people think this is based on fact, as another way to extract gold from rivers is to suspend a sheep fleece in the water. The gold fragments get caught in the wool, and if there are enough, the fleece would look golden.

What is a carat?

The purity of gold is measured in carats. Twenty-four carat gold is pure gold. Eighteen carat gold has 18/24 parts gold, 9 carat is 9/24 parts gold, and so on.

Not the vegetable!

Atomic number 80

Hg

Mercury
Metal

The old name for mercury was 'quicksilver' and its symbol comes from the Latin word 'hydragyrum', which means liquid silver. It is the only metal that is a liquid at room temperature, (the only other element that is liquid at room temperature is bromine) and it's so dense that even lead will float on it.

Thermometers used to contain mercury, but many now contain alcohol instead, as mercury is quite toxic. It is used in the silvery amalgam used to fill teeth – but it isn't toxic in this amalgam. It was used in lots of medicines before people realised how harmful it was, and is still used in many types of mascara. In Moorish Spain, some of the palace gardens had mercury reflecting-pools in them for visitors to look into (and dip their fingers into, which wasn't such a great idea).

Minamata disease

Methylmercury was released in industrial waste water into the sea near the Japanese city of Minamata between 1932 and 1968. It contaminated fish and shellfish, which were eaten by the local people, giving them mercury poisoning. Animals were also affected. In cats, it was known as 'dancing cat fever' because of the way in which their movement was affected. In humans it caused numbness, damage to hearing and speech and, in some cases, paralysis, insanity, coma and death. Over 2200 victims suffered from Minamata disease.

Mad as a hatter

If you've read *Alice in Wonderland*, you'll have come across the Mad Hatter. Lewis Carroll didn't just dream this up at random though. In Victorian times Mad Hatter Disease was well known and was caused by the use of mercury compounds in the production of felt for fur hats.

Atomic number 81

Tl

Thallium
Metal

Known as 'the poisoner's poison' because it was often used in murders. Thallium sulphate was easy to buy as it used to be sold as rat poison. It was soluble, tasteless, odourless and hard to detect in the body.

Arrrghh!

'Aunt Thally' Grills

One of Australia's most famous murder cases featured thallium poisoning. In 1953, 63-year-old Caroline Grills was convicted of killing four members of her family and trying to kill another two by putting thallium sulphate in their tea. In prison in Sydney, she was nicknamed 'Aunt Thally'. This was just one of a spate of thallium murders in Australia at that time.

Agatha Christie

Agatha Christie used thallium to kill the victims in her book *The Pale Horse*. In doing so, she also saved some real lives, as at least two readers recognised the symptoms of thallium poisoning once they had read it!

Agatha Christie

Atomic number 83
Bi
Bismuth
Metal

A silvery-pink metal, mostly obtained as a by-product of copper and tin production. Probably best known as an ingredient of some over-the-counter treatments for stomach problems.

Bismuth is also used as a pigment in nail varnish and eye shadow.

Atomic number 85
At
Astatine
Metal

One of the rarest elements on Earth, it has never actually been seen! This is because a piece big enough to be seen would vaporise in the heat generated by its radioactivity. Probably less than one gram exists on Earth at any time.

Atomic number 87
Fr
Francium
Metal

The most unstable of the natural elements, it's almost impossible to investigate, so not a lot is known about it, and it doesn't have any commercial uses.

Pb
Lead
Metal

Lead is the heaviest metal and gets its symbol from the Latin word 'plumbum'. Until fairly recently most water pipes were made of lead – this is why we call people who fix water pipes plumbers.

It was a good idea in one respect as lead is easy to mould and bend, so you can make pipes that go round corners. However it was also a very bad idea since lead is toxic. Nowadays copper is used to make pipes instead. Lead has had various uses for thousands of years because it is easy to obtain and to work.

Let me lead you through some facts about lead...

Queen Elizabeth I

Lead cosmetics

It's amazing what people will put on their faces. In the past, people used white lead in powders and pastes to give them a fashionably pale complexion, even though they knew it could lead to bad skin, baldness and even death!

Lead pigments

These were used in paints, but this has now been discontinued due to the toxicity of lead. It was a particularly bad move to paint baby cots with lead paint, as babies sometimes chew at the cot bars when they are teething.

Thomas Midgely

Thomas Midgely was an American engineer who, in 1921, discovered that adding a little tetraethyl lead to petrol made car engines work much better. Petrol manufacturers took a long time to realise that the signs of poisoning that many of their workers began to show was connected to this, but eventually scientists realised that leaded petrol was a major pollutant, affecting humans and the environment. Now, most petrol is lead-free.

Thomas Midgely may hold the unenviable record of doing more harm to the environment than any other human being, as he also developed chemicals known as CFCs, which until recently were widely used in refrigeration, aerosols and polystyrene packaging. When released into the atmosphere, these chemicals head straight for the ozone layer and hang around for thousands of years, constantly damaging it.

The Franklin Expedition

This was an Arctic exploration voyage that ended in disaster. The expedition set out from England in 1845, but never returned. Searches eventually found the remains of the expedition, including several graves. Studies of the bodies suggested that some people were poisoned by the lead which was, at the time, used to solder cans of food, but it now looks as though lots of people at that time had similar levels of lead in their bodies without suffering harm.

Pierre Curie

Marie Curie

The most highly political element in the periodic table, deadly poisonous polonium, was discovered by the Curies in 1898. They named it after their native country of Poland, in a move to publicise Poland's lack of independence at the time. The first death from polonium poisoning may have been the Curies' daughter Irene Joliot-Curie, who died from leukaemia some years after a capsule of polonium exploded on the bench where she was working.

Marie and Pierre Curie

Marie and Pierre Curie spent years studying uranium ore, and found that it contained other elements too – radium and polonium. In 1903 they were awarded the Nobel Prize for Physics, along with Henri Becquerel. Marie was the first woman ever to win one. In 1911, she was awarded another Nobel Prize – this time for Chemistry – for her work on radium (Pierre had died in 1906). She developed mobile x-ray units and drove ambulances containing them during World War I. She died of aplastic anaemia in 1934, probably as a result of her exposure to radiation. Even now, Marie Curie's notebooks are so radioactive that they have to be kept in lead lined boxes and handled by people wearing protective clothing.

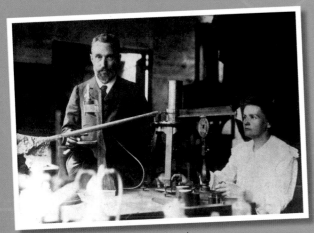

Marie and Pierre Curie working in a laboratory.

Assassinations

Polonium has been implicated in political assassinations, most famously that of Russian dissident Alexander Litvinenko in 2006. He fell ill while living in London and died a painful and lingering death in hospital. When his death was investigated traces of polonium were found in his body, and in places in London where he had been just before falling ill.

Atomic number 88

Ra
Radium
Metal

The Curies discovered radium in 1898. It is radioactive and glows in the dark. It became very popular in the early part of the 20th century, before people realised the dangers. It was used in luminous paint, particularly on watch dials. It was painted on by the so-called 'Radium Girls', who often licked their brushes to give them a nice, fine point. Not surprisingly, the girls often became ill. More bizarrely, it was added to toothpaste, hair creams and 'tonics'. Radium was also an important treatment for cancers in the early 20th century.

Atomic number 89
Ac
Actinium
Metal

It is extracted from uranium ore, but this is quite a job, since there is only about 0.2 milligrams of actinium in one tonne of ore! Because it is so scarce, not to mention highly radioactive, it has no commercial uses.

Atomic number 91
Pa
Protactinium
Metal

Very rare, very toxic, and almost entirely useless. It can be extracted – with great difficulty – from uranium ore, but 66 tons of uranium would only give you about 125 grams of protactinium!

Atomic number 90
Th
Thorium
Metal

Named after Thor, the Norse god of thunder. Some countries are researching whether this radioactive element could be used in nuclear reactors instead of uranium.

The Manhattan Project

This was the research project that developed the first atomic bombs during World War II. It involved the USA, the UK and Canada, and work was carried out at more than 30 sites in those three countries. It began in 1939, and led to the production of two types of atomic bomb: one containing uranium and the other plutonium. The project also had to monitor German research into nuclear energy, which involved agents working behind enemy lines.

The first ever nuclear explosion was the Trinity Test, carried out in New Mexico. After the test, the scientific director of the project, J Robert Oppenheimer, famously said, "Now I am become death, the destroyer of worlds" (a quote from Hindu scripture). Near the end of the war, two nuclear bombs were dropped on Japan, the only nuclear weapons ever to have been used. The Manhattan Project continued until 1947.

Atomic bomb explosion.

Atomic number 92
U
Uranium
Metal

The best known of the radioactive elements, it is used in nuclear reactors to supply electricity in many countries. Amazingly, ancient natural nuclear reactor sites have been found in Gabon, West Africa. Known as the Oklo Fossil Reactors, they were active 1.7 billion years ago!

Before it was realised it was radioactive, it was used in glazes for tiles and pottery. Its radioactivity was discovered when Henri Becquerel put a sample of uranium salts into a drawer on top of a photographic plate, and found when he looked at it later that the plate had been fogged by the radioactivity of the uranium.

Nuclear power plant.

Atomic bombs

Uranium has much more sinister uses in atomic bombs. The first atomic bomb, known as 'Little Boy', was dropped on the Japanese city of Hiroshima on August 6th 1945. The blast killed over 100,000 people. Those who died in the first few days after the bombing were mostly killed by burn or falling debris, but during the next few months, many more died of radiation sickness.

Fictional Elements

Science fiction is very keen on making up new elements. You've already met Kryptonite — here are some more.

Dilithium

The crystals that regulate the Star Ship Enterprise's warp engines in *Star Trek*.

Octiron

A dense, black metal found in the crust of Terry Pratchett's *Discworld*.

Unobtainium

The fantastically rare metal being mined on the planet Pandora in the film *Avatar*.

Mithril

A light, strong, silvery metal used by elves to make the mail shirt worn by Bilbo and Frodo Baggins in *The Hobbit* and *The Lord of the Rings*.

Carbonite

Han Solo is frozen into a block of carbonite at the end of the *Star Wars* film *The Empire Strikes Back*.

And finally... Elements which don't exist but really should.

Yummium
Chemical symbol: Mmm

The tastiest element of them all.

Amazonium

An element only available by mail order.

Gymnasium

Often added to muscle building supplements.

The Quick Particle Guide

Subatomic particles are protons, neutrons and electrons. Together these make up...

Atoms. An atom is the basic unit of an element. It can't be broken down any further by a chemical reaction. Atoms join together to make...

Molecules. Molecules are two or more atoms joined by chemical bonds. For example, an oxygen molecule is O_2 — two atoms of oxygen stuck together. Water is H_2O — two atoms of hydrogen combined with one atom of oxygen. It is a...

Compound. Compounds are substances made of molecules of two or more elements.

Above is a quick guide to the particles we've seen.

The Complete Periodic Table

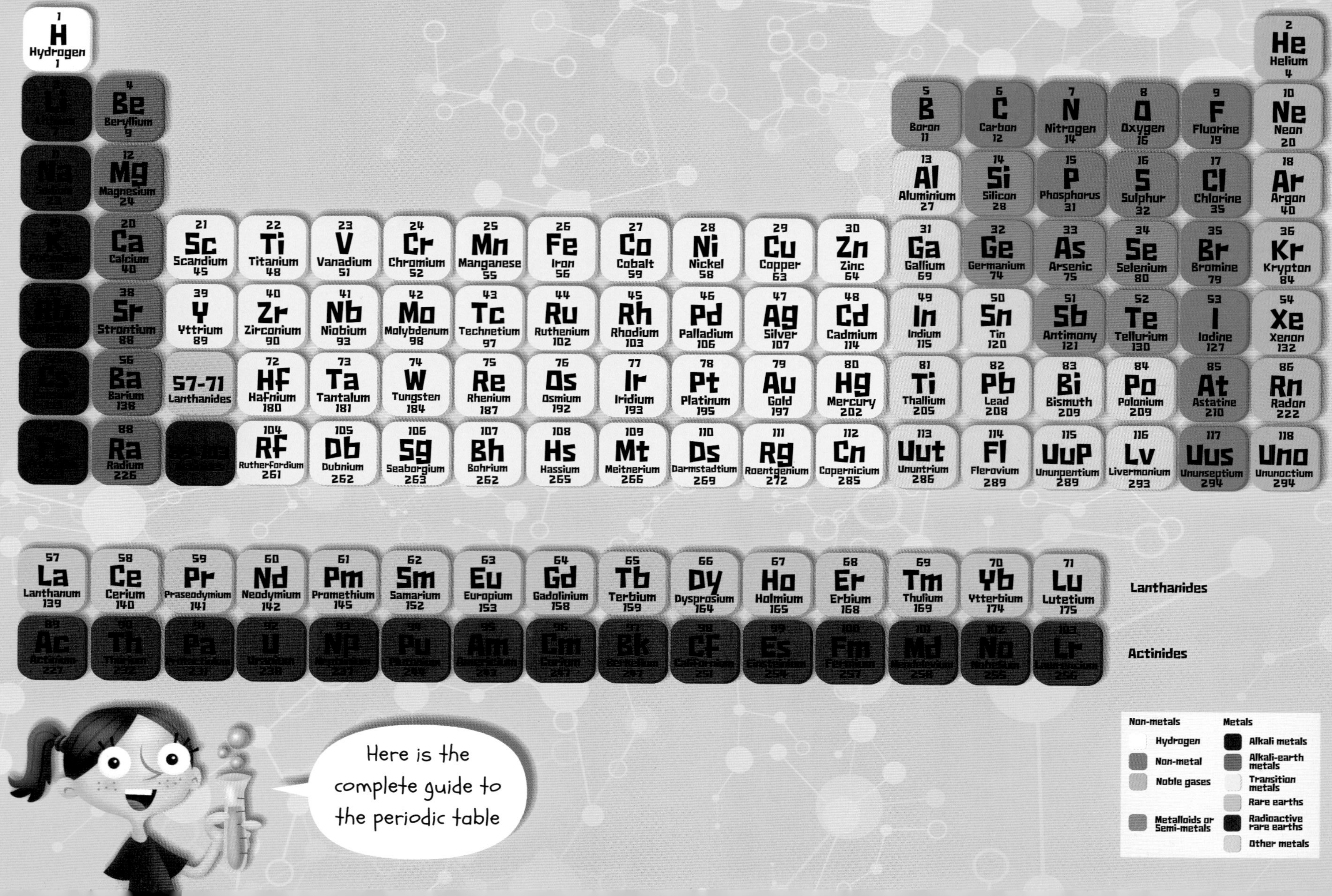

Here is the complete guide to the periodic table

Lanthanides

| 57 La Lanthanum 139 | 58 Ce Cerium 140 | 59 Pr Praseodymium 141 | 60 Nd Neodymium 142 | 61 Pm Promethium 145 | 62 Sm Samarium 152 | 63 Eu Europium 153 | 64 Gd Gadolinium 158 | 65 Tb Terbium 159 | 66 Dy Dysprosium 164 | 67 Ho Holmium 165 | 68 Er Erbium 168 | 69 Tm Thulium 169 | 70 Yb Ytterbium 174 | 71 Lu Lutetium 175 |

Actinides

| 89 Ac Actinium 227 | 90 Th Thorium 232 | 91 Pa Protactinium 231 | 92 U Uranium 238 | 93 Np Neptunium 237 | 94 Pu Plutonium 244 | 95 Am Americium 243 | 96 Cm Curium 247 | 97 Bk Berkelium 247 | 98 Cf Californium 251 | 99 Es Einsteinium 254 | 100 Fm Fermium 257 | 101 Md Mendelevium 258 | 102 No Nobelium 255 | 103 Lr Lawrencium 256 |

Main table

- 1 H Hydrogen 1
- 2 He Helium 4
- 3 Li / 4 Be Beryllium 9
- 11 Na Sodium / 12 Mg Magnesium 24
- 19 K / 20 Ca Calcium 40
- 37 Rb / 38 Sr Strontium 88
- 55 Cs / 56 Ba Barium 138
- 87 Fr / 88 Ra Radium 226

21 Sc Scandium 45	22 Ti Titanium 48	23 V Vanadium 51	24 Cr Chromium 52	25 Mn Manganese 55	26 Fe Iron 56	27 Co Cobalt 59	28 Ni Nickel 58	29 Cu Copper 63	30 Zn Zinc 64
39 Y Yttrium 89	40 Zr Zirconium 90	41 Nb Niobium 93	42 Mo Molybdenum 98	43 Tc Technetium 97	44 Ru Ruthenium 102	45 Rh Rhodium 103	46 Pd Palladium 106	47 Ag Silver 107	48 Cd Cadmium 114
57-71 Lanthanides	72 Hf Hafnium 180	73 Ta Tantalum 181	74 W Tungsten 184	75 Re Rhenium 187	76 Os Osmium 192	77 Ir Iridium 193	78 Pt Platinum 195	79 Au Gold 197	80 Hg Mercury 202
89-103 Actinides	104 Rf Rutherfordium 261	105 Db Dubnium 262	106 Sg Seaborgium 263	107 Bh Bohrium 262	108 Hs Hassium 265	109 Mt Meitnerium 266	110 Ds Darmstadtium 269	111 Rg Roentgenium 272	112 Cn Copernicium 285

- 5 B Boron 11
- 6 C Carbon 12
- 7 N Nitrogen 14
- 8 O Oxygen 16
- 9 F Fluorine 19
- 10 Ne Neon 20
- 13 Al Aluminium 27
- 14 Si Silicon 28
- 15 P Phosphorus 31
- 16 S Sulphur 32
- 17 Cl Chlorine 35
- 18 Ar Argon 40
- 31 Ga Gallium 69
- 32 Ge Germanium 74
- 33 As Arsenic 75
- 34 Se Selenium 80
- 35 Br Bromine 79
- 36 Kr Krypton 84
- 49 In Indium 115
- 50 Sn Tin 120
- 51 Sb Antimony 121
- 52 Te Tellurium 130
- 53 I Iodine 127
- 54 Xe Xenon 132
- 81 Tl Thallium 205
- 82 Pb Lead 208
- 83 Bi Bismuth 209
- 84 Po Polonium 209
- 85 At Astatine 210
- 86 Rn Radon 222
- 113 Uut Ununtrium 286
- 114 Fl Flerovium 289
- 115 Uup Ununpentium 289
- 116 Lv Livermorium 293
- 117 Uus Ununseptium 294
- 118 Uuo Ununoctium 294

Legend

Non-metals
- Hydrogen
- Non-metal
- Noble gases
- Metalloids or Semi-metals

Metals
- Alkali metals
- Alkali-earth metals
- Transition metals
- Rare earths
- Radioactive rare earths
- Other metals

Find Out More

Read

Itch (Doubleday Childrens, 2012)

A fictional adventure about Itch – an element hunter who wants to collect all of the elements in the periodic table!

Mendeleev on the Periodic Law: Selected Writings, 1869-1905 (Dover Publications, 2012)

A collection of Mendeleev's most important writings on the periodic law.

What Makes You YOU? by Gill Arbuthnott (A & C Black, 2013)

A fantastic guide to DNA, genes and everything that makes you YOU!

Visit

The Royal Scottish Museum of Scotland in Edinburgh to see the 'Restless Earth' gallery, full of fantastic specimens of rocks, meteorites and precious stones.

https://www.nms.ac.uk

The Vault in the Science Museum in London to see precious stones and meteorites.

http://www.sciencemuseum.org.uk

The Jewel Room at The Tower of London to see the fabulous precious stones set into the Crown Jewels, including part of the Cullinan diamond.

http://www.hrp.org.uk/TowerOfLondon/

Log on to

http://www.bbc.co.uk/learningzone/clips/groups-and-periods-in-the-periodic-table/10623.html

A short but informative video about the structure of the periodic table.

http://www.chem4kids.com/extras/quiz_elemintro/index.html

A great interactive quiz that will test your knowledge of the elements!

http://www.bbc.co.uk/radio4/science/puzzle4.shtml

Try out this head scratcher of a puzzle!

Glossary

Abundant Exists in a very large quantity.

Alchemist Someone who studied alchemy, which was what existed before proper, scientific chemistry. Alchemy was a combination of chemistry and magic.

Alloy A metal melted together with another element, which often makes it stronger. Bronze is an alloy of copper and tin.

Amalgam An alloy of mercury and other metals used in dental fillings.

Anaesthetic A substance that stops you feeling pain.

Annexe An extension to the main part of, in this case, the periodic table. (It's where the Lanthanides are shown).

Atom The smallest unit of an element. It is tiny in size and is made up of a positively charged nucleus surrounded by negatively charged electrons.

Atomic number The number of protons in an element.

Commercial use Use of something in order to make money. For instance, one commercial use of aluminium is to make soft drink cans.

Compound Atoms of two or more elements joined together to make molecules.

Conductor A material that carries (conducts) electricity.

Corrosion The gradual destruction of metal, caused by a chemical reaction with its environment.

Electron Particle outside the nucleus of an atom which has negative charge.

Fossil fuel Any fuel that is formed by natural processes (from plant or animal remains) – coal, gas and oil.

Galvanising Coating a metal with zinc in order to protect it from corrosion.

Group Column in the periodic table.

Haemoglobin A chemical in red blood cells that allows them to carry oxygen.

In vitro fertilisation Fertilisation outside the body. Eggs and sperm are mixed in a glass dish.

Isolated Alone – not near to anything else.

Isotopes Forms of the same element with different numbers of neutrons in the nucleus. For example, strontium has 50 neutrons, but radioactive strontium-90 has 52.

Large Hadron Collider A huge particle accelerator in Switzerland. It is used to smash particles – beams of protons, for instance – into each other at great speed to test theories about physics and try to find evidence for the existence of fundamental particles such as the Higgs Boson.

Laxative A medicine used to make it easier to empty your bowels (in other words, something that makes you poo).

Metalloid An element with properties of both a metal and a non-metal.

Mixture Different elements or compounds that are physically close together but not chemically joined.

Neutron Particle in the nucleus of an atom which has no charge.

Noble Gases A group of elements that are extremely unreactive.

Ore Mineral from which metal is extracted.

Period Row in the periodic table.

Philosopher's Stone One of the things that Alchemists tried to make (unsuccessfully). It was meant to give the maker eternal life and allow them to turn metals like lead into gold.

Photosynthesis The process by which plants use energy from sunlight to convert water and carbon dioxide into sugars.

Pigment A substance used to give something colour.

Proton Particle in the nucleus of an atom which has positive charge.

Salary A wage that is paid monthly. From the Latin word for salt – sal – as Roman soldiers got part of their pay to buy salt.

Smelt Melt ore in order to produce metal.

Solder Join pieces of metal together.

Subatomic Part of an atom.

Supernovae Huge, very bright exploding stars.

Theoretical Believed to be possible but so far lacking evidence to support that belief.

Toxic Poisonous.

Transatlantic Across the Atlantic Ocean – for example, from the UK to America.

Index

actinium 8, 56
airships 12, 13
alloys 29, 33, 37, 39, 44, 45
aluminium 9, 24, 29
antimony 9, 40
argon 9, 10
arrowheads 25
arsenic 9, 34
astatine 9, 51
atomic bombs 56, 57
atoms 6, 10, 12, 59
atomic number 9

barium 8, 41
beryllium 8, 18
Big Bang 12, 14, 19
bismuth 9, 51
blood 21, 31, 34
boron 9, 19
bromine 9, 35, 48
burning 12–13, 20, 24, 26

cadmium 9, 37
caesium 8, 41
calcium 8, 17, 28
cancer 15, 35, 42, 45, 54, 55
carat 47
carbon 16–17
carbon dioxide 11, 17
catalytic converters 37
cerium 8, 42
CFCs 53
charge 10
chemical symbol 9
chlorine 9, 17, 27
chromium 8, 29
cobalt 9, 32
compounds 11, 15, 16, 18, 32, 40, 59
conductors 16, 25, 34, 35
copper 9, 33, 51
corrosion 29, 31, 36, 39, 44
crystals 23, 35, 39
Curie, Marie and Pierre 54

diamonds 16, 23, 35
dye 34, 35
dysprosium 9, 43

electrons 10, 12
element, definition of 6
erbium 9, 43
europium 8, 42
Exotic States of Matter 11

explosives 18, 41

families of elements 7
fertilisers 18, 28
fluorine 9, 17, 22
fossil fuels 12, 17
francium 8, 51
Franklin Expedition 53
fuels 12

gadolinium 9, 32, 43
gallium 9, 33
gases, definition of 11
germanium 9, 34
gold 9, 37, 46–47
graphite 16
Greenhouse Effect 17
groups 8
gunpowder 27

hafnium 8, 44
helium 9, 12, 13, 14, 15
holmium 9, 43
human body 17
hydrogen 8, 11, 12–13, 17, 28, 59

identifying elements 6
indium 9, 39
iodine 9, 40
iridium 9, 45
iron 9, 17, 30–31, 32, 42

jewellery 32, 33, 37, 38, 45, 46

krypton 9, 15

lanthanides 42–43
lanthanum 8, 42
Large Hadron Collider 14
laughing gas 18
laxatives 40
lead 16, 36, 39, 48, 52–53, 54
liquid nitrogen 18
liquids, definition of 11
lithium 8, 19
lutetium 9, 43

magnesium 8, 17, 24
magnetic 21, 32, 42, 43
manganese 8, 32
Manhattan Project 56
mass 10
Mendeleev, Dmitri 6–7, 29, 34, 36
mercury 48–49

Midgely, Thomas 53
Minamata disease 49
minerals 24, 32, 35
mining 16, 32, 39
mirrors 38
mixtures 11
molecules 11, 14, 20, 21, 59
molybdenum 8, 36
mustard gas 27

natural elements 6
natural gas 14
neodymium 8, 42
neon 10, 15
neutrons 10
nickel 9, 32, 37, 42
niobium 8, 36
nitrogen 9, 11, 17, 18
Nobel Prize 54
Noble Gases 15
Northern Lights 21
nuclear fusion 13
nuclear reactors 36, 43, 56, 57
nucleus 10

Oklo Fossil Reactors 57
ore 30, 34, 36, 56
osmium 9, 45
oxygen 9, 11, 17, 20–21, 31, 36, 43, 59
ozone 20, 53

paint 13, 32, 37, 38, 42, 52, 55
palladium 9, 37
panning 46
periodic table 7, 8–9, 15
periods 8
petrol 53
pewter 39
phosphorus 9, 17, 26
photography 24, 38, 57
photosynthesis 20, 24, 45
plasma 11
platinum 9, 43, 45
plutonium 8, 56
poison 34, 40, 49, 50, 52–55
polonium 9, 54–55
potassium 8, 17, 27, 28
praseodymium 8, 42
predictions 7
promethium 8, 42
properties 7
protactinium 8, 56
protons 10, 12

radiation 20
radioactive 15, 35, 36, 41, 42, 51, 54–57
radium 8, 54, 55
radon 9, 15
reactive 19, 26, 35, 41

reading the periodic table 8–9
rhenium 8, 44
rhodium 8, 37
rubidium 8, 35
rust 31
ruthenium 9, 36

salt 22–23
samarium 8, 42
scandium 8, 29
selenium 9, 34
skunk 26
silicon 9, 17, 25
silly putty 19
silver 9, 34, 38, 45
singularity 12
sodium 8, 17, 22–23
solids, definition of 11
stars 16, 18
States of Matter 11
steel 29, 31, 39
strontium 8, 35
subatomic particles 12, 59
sulphur 9, 17, 26–27
sun 13, 20

tantalum 8, 44
technetium 8, 36
tellurium 9, 40
terbium 9, 43
thallium 9, 50
thorium 8, 56
thulium 9, 43
tin 9, 33, 39, 51
titanium 8, 29
toxic 26, 34, 37, 40, 48, 52, 56
tungsten 8, 44

unreactive 15
uranium 55, 57

vanadium 8, 29

weights 7, 8
Wonder, Stevie 21
World Wars 13, 26, 27, 54, 56

x-ray 43, 54
xenon 9, 15

ytterbium 9, 43
yttrium 8, 35

zinc 9, 17, 31, 33, 34
zirconium 8, 35, 44